STONES HOLD WATER

poems by

ZAKIA R. KHWAJA

Finishing Line Press
Georgetown, Kentucky

STONES HOLD WATER

Publisher: Leah Huete de Maines
Editor: Christen Kincaid
Cover Art: Anderson Photography
Author Photo: Scott Leonard Studios
Cover Design: Elizabeth Maines McCleavy

Order online: www.finishinglinepress.com
        also available on amazon.com

Author inquiries and mail orders:
Finishing Line Press
P. O. Box 1626
Georgetown, Kentucky 40324
U. S. A.

Table of Contents

Dedicated to my grandparents:
Khwaja Mohammad Murtaza and Maqbool Jahan Begum
S. Abul Hassan Jafri and Ishrat Jahan Begum

THE MANGO TREE

I

The villagers mark time
by the angle of the mango tree's
shadow across the square.

Its roots pulse like arteries under the village.

II

The elders argue politics, land
feuds and progress under
the leafy canopy. Mango slivers,
plucked from ice buckets, disappear
under drooping mustaches,
peels sucked white and clean.

The men work the fields.

III

Nearby, over mud-clay walls,
the women gossip, squalling
burdens clutched to hips.
Toddlers trip towards the chickens.
Fresh-rinsed dupattas flutter
in the breeze—crimson, orange, blue!
All breathe deep the air, redolent
with the incense of mango chutneys,

fruit-flesh bubbling on brick stoves.

IV

Impatient with writing slates,
sling-shotting comrades, we stare
longingly at the succulent fruit

bending the branches.

The teacher and the bees drone.

V

Every summer the tree grows
that one juicy, unblemished mango—
perfectly pulp-fattened.
How to sneak up and pin a name-slip
on that king of fruits? The race
to get the golden trophy.

Sometimes, the crows get to it first.

VI

Still, sticky evenings,
we corner Old Nani-Ma
on sun-toasted charpoys
till she spins dreams of sorcerers and
djinns, whose souls can be wrung

out of parrots sitting in mango trees.

LORE

At dusk, the women come to the courtyard
between the huts and cast stories around the fire
feeding on the slow roast of their days. Time to forget

the heavy sun they carried for hours,
rattling in dry pitchers, until they flushed it out
at the nearest well two villages away. Now,

in the night, they pull thorns from their tread
and tuck secrets down each other's breasts
while the men sleep off moonshine and truck shifts.

The crones pass on their lives to the tribe
and teach gypsy girls how to curve flesh against
stropping desert winds without mislaying themselves.

Clan songs of dusty lands with vulture skies
lift off the drum and swirl into constellations.

MAGHREB

"Tie back your hair" my abbess-strict
grandmother orders. "Day in farewell
to Night is the heavy hour when djinns
possess maidens with unbound locks."

Why should they not
fix their whispers in the black fall
of my tresses, their smokeless fire
directing my touches, the banked surges
of my body finally unloosed
from all the knots holding me in place?

Heedless, eyes lashed to the sky, comb arrested
midstroke between birdsong and cricket call,
I watch the last aureate streak fade to twilight—
the path of a demon-lover crossing the dusk,
searching for me.

DANCING BEHIND CLOSED DOORS

It begins with shedding disguises:

Balled-up dupattas kicked
to the edge of carpets.

Passion unleashed
in the arch of hips.

Sweat between thighs and breasts
patches up spines buried
in the length of backs.

Loosened plaits
and melody-drunk

soles, bold

until a man clears his throat
on the other side of the wall.

Our feet go cold.

DIRTY LAUNDRY

I come awake in the sweaty embrace
of last night's mistake to the slap,
slap, slap of wet cloth on stone slabs—

syncopating river ragas that dawn
with the maajhi's love song. Fog,
gray as stray dogs, shrinks into alleys.

Women measure out the river with ghee canisters
while urchins squeal among the shallows. Tossing dirty
jokes the men scrape at curry stains with fingernails.

Cheap dyes tint lather from homemade soaps.
Saris unravel their greens and golds. Collars,
sheets and pillowcases smut-purged, sag

against a sky free of clouds as dhobis
with crinkled palms scare off kingfishers.

THE CURTAIN

The scarlet rag catches
my eye as I turn on the street,
body raw from selling stale nights
to spent men on sandpaper sheets.
It flirts with the dawn
like a practiced tease.
On still days it sighs
by the high window frame.

Beyond the tangle of cable and concrete,
the hem beats against the worn brick.
In this back lane, where the city is faded,
the addicts and the homeless
blow kisses to its electric sheen.

Once, from behind the peek-a-boo slit,
I heard a woman giggle. It set the alley
dogs howling, who in all this time,
had forgotten how to bark.
I look everyday
for the face behind the laugh.

JHAROKA

Three evenings, you and I have
emptied our shoes of desert sand and
leaned against the Rajasthani balcony that hovers
over dune valleys and camel trails—
an Alif Layla Wa Layla magic carpet.

We need this pink city at seven stories,
between sun glare and darkness, and time
to unmask the quiet behind the distant
chatter of nine-to-five days.

Cushioned against the world, you
follow a map of rivers and I
bind verses into raft logs. The hookah
gurgles in the silence, slides from one wall
to the other, charcoal in our mouths.
We will kiss the smoky taste away

when the moon is no longer a fingernail
edge jammed in a palm but a white-hot scythe
slivering our nakedness and
the dry wind brings the rasps
of gypsies to our bed.

We lie face-to-face and stuff
pillows with secrets. Slowly, knit
the night a net of fractured stars.

THE MOON IS A ﻥ

tonight—a thin curve
with a star unsteady
in the gravity
of its embrace.

Within the crescent
of your arms, I rise
to your stone

lips, suck
in a lost breath:
you have me
and I, you devil,

have nothing
but your sickle-horned
silhouette.

ALL NIGHT, HER HAIR

twist upon the sheets, under and over our trunks,
my arms tendriled vines, thick with ebony snakes.
At first light, the coils will slacken and follow her
off my chest as she straightens her spine, takes
two continents and an ocean in stride, leaves

me with midnight strands in my fist.
Her hair hangs in long ropes that catch at my neck,
bind me to her nakedness. We have promised
to fall out of love, come dawn. How will I ever
forget the monsoon in her eyes?

Tomorrow, she will snap elastics around the snarls,
peg up the wild tips, poker face in place, but tonight,
she is unraveled disarray, spilling
in silken skeins across the bed as we pretend
this is enough.

PAPER BOATS

You and I, on opposite banks of the Atlantic,
have shored and scuttled this connection
through the deep years—
every time we think it lost to the prudence
of halting words, it buoys up, dangerous
as the sneaker-currents that drag the coastline
towards restricted waters. We come and go
in broken waves, neither able to find
anchor in the other—you cannot promise
to stay and I cannot pace my shore forever so
today, when the sky rains oceans
I fold poems into paper boats
and float them into the future the way
children entrust origami skiffs
to roadside rivulets in the hope that when
the high seas between our hearts rise
to submerge all bridges,
in the lonely recede you will come
upon the flattened hulls and creased sails,
brush the silt off my words
and raise them to your lips.

CUSTODIAN OF REMAINS

A young couple has moved into the Purani Haveli, where
fallen branches and dandelion weeds no longer choke
the serpentine drive. The shock of roses,
roses everywhere. I am still unmended
from our time.

My eyes travel up the creeper, now restrained
with twine, to the second floor balcony and I wonder
if they are bedding in the room where you and I
spent every night that moony month of June.

Remember, when we scared the watchman on purpose?
The next day he spoke of the manic laughter of witches.
My mouth longs for your kisses.

After you left for foreign streets, chasing dreams
bigger than the village, I roamed the lanes, waiting
for letters that never came. I have given up
being the custodian of remains. Know,
that even the ruins have been taken.

HUSK

In the end, it takes everything—
all that I am—to close
the door on you, my perfect

storm. Palms flat against
the heavy bolt, I lean into
the aching labor of pressing

you out of my heart, yoked
to this Herculean task until
threshold, stoop, the final whoosh

of your hissed egress like a demon
dispossessed of the body that is now
a cracked husk on the floor.

THE HOLLOW MEN

Every evening, he and I drink the sun low—

raise glasses to our shadows dancing
on the tavern walls before we slump
like wrung out washing on a clothesline.

One day, I ask him what remains of what
he lost and see time ripple in his far stare,
the way a sandpiper skimming low disturbs

the stillness of a lake. He closes his eyes
on a sigh and lifts his nose to the air as if breathing
the perfumed sillage of a lover passing near.

He speaks of secret letters received through the hands
of friends, carried in his breast-pocket for days
and his voice holds the tremor of rabab strings

still holding the sorrow of a fading ballad.
For a heartbeat, he is youth and yearning stirred
before settling into the dregs of his drained cup.

THE NAME OF LOVE

The dust cloud swells into a regiment
of high-turbaned kinsmen with flat,
gunmetal eyes. I tremble between his arms—
summer leaf sere before its time.

Not a daughter, I am the House of Honor.
Not a son, he is the House of Pride.
The feudals come, talons extended—
Old World raptors slavering
to pick clean their shamed prestige
from our flesh.
Brothers, uncles, fathers.
Butchers, butchers, butchers.

I lash myself to his chest as they split open
the seal of skin on skin. We splinter
like a ship's mast struck
by lightening. As we receive the unforgiving
hurricane of bone and blade,
our names pass into epic tales that spread
across the plains and leap to tongues
whenever they couple doomed
love and mad rebellion.

MOSQUITO NET

To this day, our elders nurse the sting:

A favorite son forsook the tribe, his blood
gone white, he let the enemy in
through the fortifications, bribed
with honeyed women. They swarmed
over our gold and grain, sucked the flame
from our hearths. Pale, at the plague he
had unleashed, the son flew with them,
only to be found the next day—staked
in a field, thorax curved over abdomen—
lifeless as a bee after cruel children pin it.

Seasons of empty follow—wintering
hives starve and buzzards come to roost.
The elders have nothing but lessons
to trickle into the mouths of young.
Every child in the tribe knows: to loot
a honey tree, you have to follow a honey bee.

Decades later, my cousins and I learn
blood ties beneath an ochroid mosquito net until
we can trace every thread in the mesh.
Buzzy afternoons, we sit shoulder-to-shoulder
and recite genealogies from the shajra-nasab, recall
family scandals: clan feuds, elopements, bastard
daughters and sons, the mad uncle who hunted
shadows with a BB gun. Within the net, honey
drips from our chins. The enemy dashes
against the tight weave, thirsty for a taste.

STONES HOLD WATER

I learn dolomite before doll,
gripping my father's fingers
as we wade into the heart of rocks.

An ocean beats in all of us,

he says, dripping lithified
shells from his pockets.

He hands me a rose
quartz and curls my fist
around the universe
within a petrified star-

fish. The truth of mountains is:

They will become pebbles
on windowsills.

FADING

Nine decades hobble Baba's legs, halt
his walks to the jasmine shrub.
The scent of Spring fades from our wrists and plaits.

He no longer paces the drive late night to switch
on his glare as we try to sneak up the stairs.
Bruises appear as we trip in the dark.

He grows faint in the library, the way handwriting
lightens on the back of sepia photographs and
our evenings lose their stars.

It bothers him when he vanishes from the prayer mat.
That day he remains chin-sunk on the sofa.
In his place, we offer ourselves to God.

He shrinks, pulling his edges in, shucking off
the world until he is a kernel, ready
to be planted. We step into his empty shoes.

MY GRANDMOTHER'S GEESE

Dadi-Ma inspects the undersides of our shoes
if she imagines a footprint in the podina patch:
Only her precious long-beaked geese
can uproot the paneeri.

That, too, is our fault.

The vicious fowls arrow-straighten their necks
parallel to the ground and chase us off the lawn.
My cousin's calves barely escape their snaps.

Ruling the roost, they bar us
from the clubhouse, the cricket pitch,
and cackle at us from Dadi-Ma's lap.

Two policemen, the chowkidar and the gardener comb
the streets for three geese till nightfall. Guileless, we wonder
who left the gate open. Dadi-Ma will never know

a sweeper's family ate roast today.

SARSON

I

Lemon sunshine and beyond high
open-mesh fences, mustard blooms
till the horizon. We answer the call
of riotous abandon.

The driver must stop the bus.

II

Six university friends and I pounce
off the fence railing into the thick
spread of chick-down petals, leaving
spreadeagled depressions

in a field of yolk-tipped stalks.

III

Armpits full of sarson, we deer-
leap towards each other in slow
motion, enacting Bollywood
reunions of separated lovers.

The girls tuck mustard sprigs
behind their ears. Years later,
the scent will powder their nose
from the pages of a book.

The boys stick twigs through buttonholes.

IV

Sunlight strikes off the arcing
scythe. A turban pokes

through the froth of sarson:
The farmer is upon us.

V

Blossoms and leaves
catch at us as we whoop towards
the fence. We jump it and shed
a golden trail of petals.

The pollen rubbed into our jeans
never washes out.

ARMOR

Kaala daana never goes into our meals.

Nani-Ma flings a handful of the seeds
in a skillet and us grandchildren troop
into the kitchen. Three times the pan circles
our torsos. The fumes settle within

the trenches of scalp and skin, ready
to slay the foreign invasion of ill will.
We watch heat breach the ebony grains
that spit and writhe as if possessed by djinns.

She raises an army of smoke assassins
from every pellet to fortify us against any evil
eye ever cast in our direction. Chests puffed,
shoulders back, braced for battle, we believe

we are invincible, armored in smoke.

JIDDOJOHAD

I read the Roznama Jang
to my grandfather's cataracts—
seer-white in sunlight.

"JIDDojohad, not JADDojohad," he corrects
as my eleven years struggle with the careful Urdu
of journalists, while beneath our feet
a secret basement press hums
words dying on tongues, welted off backs,
choked into cuffed hands.

A bulb sparks over democratized
print, ink-smudged fingers screw clean
from acetone-soaked muslin. Man-high piles
of foolscap lean against foundations. I learn

how to crease sentences into books
that get transported in the hushed dark
by tarp-covered wheelbarrows.

BURNING OF THE BOOKS

The skies do not rain
the night of the bonfire.

The pyre stacks ten feet high
with flammable texts.

The people are invited by the mad
mullahs, not taking no for an answer.

Ash-grayed hair, tear-blanched eyes,
faces black with shame, we witness:

A scientist, scorched skinless, trying
to rescue a universe of possibility.

A professor, head ablaze, frantic to save
the beingness of outlawed thinking.

A writer, clutching the remnants
of inspired invention in a charred fist.

A student, burning with questions
for the men who raze down a pyramid

of books with one hand, hold
the Quran in the other.

SCRIPTIO INFERIOR

Hejazi Arabic lies
in implacable oil-black
over the watery cursive that undulates
like the Indus across the parchment.

Mullahs scraped the vellum
to make room for dictated script, but
here and there, ancient characters
call through the bars
of alif-laam-meems
even as dark acid chews at their lips.

The palimpsest doublespeaks
through war and peace.
Centuries cannot unlayer it.

NASTALIQ

Cat-lazy afternoons, my lead-smudged
fingers trace nastaliq script—a fusion of curling,
arcing Persian and geometric Kufic Arabic.

Straight-backed *alif*, big-bellied *chey*, the *qaaf*—
vocalized deep in the uvula—harsh, unlike the softer
kaaf; I give a turban to *tey*, a bindiya to *zwad*,

thinking of calligraphy in a Sadeqain, Faiz ghazals
sung by Noor Jehan, rhyming riddles and my grandfather
reading Urdu poetry, quizzing me on poets' names.

Absorbed in eternal lines of nastaliq, entranced
like mystic sufis, I decipher God and Love and
Self until the sweaty, blunted pencil slants.

THE MAD HOURS

He sits at the desk in a puddle
of candlelight: drenched god sweating

the birthing of worlds. In the corner,
between the frame and the door, a spider

knits a new home and rats pull the stuffing
out of pillows while his eyes burn and

hands poke at shadows with inksticks.
Come morning, he will count

wax-gilded moth wings.

WRITING ON WATER

I

Salutes of cannon mean
nothing to the old woman
clawing at the ice
hardening her son's grave.

II

At the kitchen table, a bride swirls
curlicues through water rings
from sweating bottles of Chardonnay.

She writes his name in fluid
strokes and watches the lines merge
before dripping off the border.

Raindrops rat-a-tat against the windows.

III

Fog tunnels through the street, thick
as discharge from a cannon's muzzle.

She tries to keep
the car from moving—
nose and palm flat
against the window.

The soldier on the other side
draws two dots above
an orphan U
within his circle of breath
on the glass.

She wears his brave face
as the portrait breaks—
eyes streaking down towards the smile.

MIGRATION 1947

Beneath the mound   of tangled limbs
and gaping jugulars   orphaned Azadi

cat-senses   prowling   looting Sikhs
slicing through the forest   of passengers

trains arrived in Karachi   no one alive   no
one alive   she   storm-rent leaf   flung

from native trees   hopeful   of seeding
a new country   raw borders   weeping

on white sahib maps   independence-drunk
mobs   torch villages   bare feet collect thorns

in the flight   to liberty   she shuts her eyes
screams   when the train stops   and

hands   reach for her   Land of the Pure
she comes   with nothing

but the life   kicking   beneath her ribs

SIRENS

My mother, vacationing from schools-turned-emergency
centers, dead fainted when a cousin returned, flag
and body bag delivered as sirens blared for the last
time before peace was signed. The airstrikes of '65—
spiraling alizarin stars from smoked-flesh skies.
She would tiptoe behind windows painted black,
dousing table lanterns. Her uncle patrolled the streets
ensuring no errant pinpricks of light became bullseyes
for IAF Gnats. Foghorn sirens announced Dadi-Ma,
Quran on head and jewel box in armpit, huffing to sit
under the oak table. Baba's *"Allahu Akbar, Allahu Akbar"*
tranquilized nerves. Fifty years later, my mother, worrying
her rosary, starts and pales as the siren heralding the Ramzan
fast punctures skies lightening from obsidian to cobalt.

DREAMERS OF THE HILLS

For Kashmir

Once again curfews shutter the valley of markhor and saffron.
The sour sharpness of snipers and stone-pelters, teargassers and
pellet-dodgers thickens borders. Barred behind windows we mourn

as jungle crows and turtle doves take flight from the chenar tops.
Our waterfalls run rust from yesterday's veins. Some days, in rebellion,
we escape up hillsides and on summer evenings rest our shoulders against

the stone edging of mountain roads. Sweat drips off our bared necks
as we gaze, upside down, at home-pyres far below. Nights smoke
with ashed futures as we dream of galaxies far from armies, pretend

bootprints are not appearing on our throats and our slopes
are not choked with soldiers. In freedom, there had been no sting
deeper than the slice of wind across our jugulars.

THE AIR IS VERMILION

Red mud churns
in rivers plugged
with bloated cadavers—
face down, belly up,
the corpses of children.

The air is vermilion
with smoke-dense spires—
villages and towns afire:
Life, thin. Forsaken.

The living stumble
in salmon mists rising
from blood-sodden earth.
Wet soles drag footprints
through crusted, saturated dirt.

Staggering, ankle-deep—
The skies no longer
accept the innocent.

THE BROKEN GOD

*On December 16, 2014 Tehrik-e-Taliban Pakistan attacked the
Army Public School in Peshawar and killed 147 people.
132 were students.*

I am placing alabaster Zeus
on the top shelf, one eye
on the TV screen, when
the camera cuts

to a shredded textbook, a school
wall pitted with bullets,
the begging-bowl hands
of a mother collecting tears,

a father clutching a bloody shoe
to his chest. In a hospital hallway,
a policeman waits with a stack
of half-sized coffins—the nation's future
in intensive care units.

I quake and Zeus separates
from his pedestal—clean break
at the ankles. He topples
and hides his face in the carpet.

TAXILA MUSEUM

Lotus-positioned with stupas and chipped
Gandhara pottery, dozens of Buddhas enlighten.
Teaching patience, benign Siddhartas

sit in abhayamudra, rib-jutting Gautamas
fast in dhyana, enduring with slight smiles.
Third eye chiseled into foreheads.

We bring all the lives behind us to all the lives
behind them, stand reflected in the glassy
amnion like so many prop roots of the same banyan.

Outside, the world continues to break
in whoops of hate, but here, in shatterproof
silence we piece stucco back to bone, hold

on to stone. The idol-lords of Dharmarajika
and Sirkup, eyes pressed shut, create monastic
dreamscapes, while still others take the watch.

Shelf-small statues, pillar-long faces bless
heritage organizations giving them sanctuary—
The Buddhas of Bamiyan are dust in the valley.

THE FESTIVAL OF SNAKES

I

Milk stands in bowls,
cream-skins pinched
off for the greedy serpent
gods who will be paraded
through the forecourt
by the worshippers.

Within the temple, the spectacle
of miracles costs a garland.
Outside, the priests stage elaborate
exorcisms for poor souls, who bray
at the door, cattle-supplicant
to any hand that will grant relief
from wilting crops, leaky roofs, disease.
They should have prayed harder, stayed
on their knees, now life is the tyranny
of one moment after the other—they come,
savings chinking in desperate palms.

No one pays attention
to the hissing boy
with the darting tongue.

II

The crowd constricts
around the sapera
with the curved spine,
his chunri turban—a coiled
red-spotted diadem snake.

The miracles of soothsayers,
witch-doctors, acrobats on stilts pales
as the snakeman's pungi resurrects

the drained naga twisting
in the woven basket. It rises, onyx
backbone contorting to nasal strains.
The snake gods have promised us rain.

The handler puts on a show:
the slit-mouth sinks its empty fangs
into the muscled arm.

My crops are wilting.
I will believe anything.

DEAD CROWS

Slack
puppet men droop
hand-lopped
from electricity poles
like dead

crows welded
by rain to faulty power
lines, strung up as if vaunting
a butcher's shop.

SEEN

I notice
one of their child-folk today:
empty dinnerplate gaze,
bony fingers grasping
at my coattails. The rest
is sunken skin.

I hear
they exist at the interstice
of death and life—their language,
plaintive. If you roll back the concrete
edge of palaces, you can find
whole colonies swept under rich
patterns, peeking up
through tasseled fringes.
They crouch like dung
beetles on the refuse
thrown from turrets and
if you look them in the eye
you never sleep again.

I snag on the child, risen
from a crack in the sidewalk,
unflattened by careless
moccasins. I see her

and now I see them all.

GAMBLE

Whose head will roll tomorrow?

The feudals raise hands and titter
behind signet rings. Their ladies

have made it the fashion to hide
their throats under heavy chokers

while the sardars fold extra starch
into their cravats. They banquet

on choice cuts from the day's hunt
and place bets on the peasants sharpening

their knives against the gates,
that they will never storm in for their flesh.

THE PAYMENT

Her beam dims forever when
the father who always angled

his shoulders between her
and mountain gusts releases

her from the folds of his chador
into the lap of the village elder

with the arctic stare. Her doll
is not part of the debt settlement and

has to be left behind with her mother,
who with snuffed-candle eyes, remembers

gnarled hands on young thighs.

DRESS CODE

After my thirteenth birthday, Mother puts all my shorts
and skirts and sleeveless shirts in the giveaway bin while
I am shoved into a training bra with biting straps.

A woman must not move beneath her clothes.

The leftover trousers and jeans are sanctioned, provided
I wear them baggy with tent blouses that square my slight curves.

A woman must be hidden from the lustful gaze of men.

Under fabric, I dissolve—a snail, coated in salt.
My brother—shirtless, flaunting shorts, is indifferent.

A woman must not invite attention.

Between neckline and hemline, men pinch me in the bazaars.
We do not speak of my reddened parts.

A woman must observe decorum.

Behind the school wall, the police find my shalwar.
They find me gagged with my own dupatta.
What was I wearing at the time of the incident?

VITRIOLAGE

Acid sizzled off
my nose, burnt furrows
down my chin. I can see
my teeth through the hole
in my cheek. My sin

was a dowry of steel pots.
My husband expected
land-plots, a car, at the very least,
a TV. Still, he showed mercy—
it could have been

death-by-gas-stove.
There is nowhere to go:

My parents shrink
from the black
and blue in my skin.

SILENCE TURNING SHOUT

Fingertips pick at lips,
releasing words banished
to the back of throats,
voices under house arrest emerge.
Tongues freely taste language.
Whispers meet at street corners,
beggar-jaw to rebel-ear, while
tea shop gossips pass intelligence
with the croissants and dissent
stomps into the back rooms of restaurants.
Table-top speeches crowd into pamphlets.

The establishment of censorship shuts
mouths, brings muzzles out but
silence has already turned to shout no
more, no more. Concave bellies bare
teeth at the feasting lords of greed
while newspaper boys hawk revolution
at intersections and pundits bet
the fate of a nation on the power
of slogans and pickets.

MARGALLA DAWN

A Eurasian Wild Boar considers me,
eyes half-closed, chewing a lantana camara sprig,
rolling it around in his maw like a don with a cigar.

He stamps a cloven hoof on the forest floor.
He has generational settlements here but we find
the hills hard to share. History
dangles its poisoned vine between us:

> In the 80s, twenty thousand pig tails were mailed in to a Punjab
> government office the first year it granted rewards for porcine hunting.
> In the 90s, the army smoked ten thousand boars in a single operation.

Could this garbage-looter's ancestors been some of them?
Was it a revenge attack when a hiker was gored?
What about all the traffic accidents they cause
when they descend from the hills onto our roads?

I once saw his kind bulldoze into a Suzuki van
and crater in the passenger door. The driver had perforated
its skull with an AK-47 before it had another go.

What am I without a weapon?

He considers me as if marking which ribs
to slide between. I am thin skin and sweat.
Should I heft a fallen branch? He spits
the sprig and I can count the teeth in his yawning mouth.

LUCIFERIN

A winged light-bringer, burning
the Day Star at its end, winks

through crepuscular rays.
All of night cannot mute

the brilliant cursor pulsing
at the base of grass-blades, appearing

in the shadowy triangles between
the maple leaves, now, a pin

jabbing at its golden reflection
in a puddle, pulling me to its alluring

halo until it hooks on my hair and
I flick it to the pavement.

GIANT IMPACT

The Giant Impact Theory postulates that a rogue planet Orpheus smashed obliquely into Earth, the dust and debris from the impact coalesced far from the Earth's gravitational pull and resulted in the formation of the Moon. The collision completely destroyed Orpheus.

Terra glows, her young body dances
on the starlit floor, and not all the chaos

of the universe can stop Orpheus from gravitating
to her side. They are ill-matched:

She wants to settle down, he is nothing
but a rogue wanderer. Their incendiary affair

changes their worlds forever. Unable to alter
his ways, he crashes and burns. Shattered

by his suicide, for a while, her own life hangs
in the balance until she finds she is with child.

Then her dolorous vapors become joyous rivers
and her lava fields subside to fertile valleys.

She is mother, creation teems in her gather.
But what of the child? She thrives,

all eyes pulled to her gentle light—
poets, wolves, ocean-tides...

The silver lining in our darkest hours.

LAKE TAPESTRY

Blue-warp, gold-weft
watered silk pegged
taut with reeds.

The sun stitches
copper and scarlet
sequins to the weave

of minnow and bluegill.
Shallows breathe in
shadows hemmed with

katydids and froglets.
Before evening stains
the trees, a kingfisher

rips through
the tapestry for a last meal.

CLARITY

I

I can no longer escape
under summer's beachy
carapace. When did winter
creep up on me and the sun go
weak in my embrace?

II

The storm is snapping
up the horizon.

Warmth leaches from me
like steam from a doused fire,
fogging the white-on-white
landscape, staking deeper
the icicles in my chest.
Chills interrupt breaths.

III

I'm going under

waves—smoke trails
of a thousand released
genies curl beneath
a pane of cold clarity.

YEAR END

Snow blunts the rises and chickadees skip
cheeps. Flowers pale away, interred in caskets
of clotted grass. Aspens, stand skeletal and
sucked under leached skies. At the window,

I wring my hands—another year passing,
wired to screens that inflict news
of war and disease. Remote after phone after remote
after phone, a holding pattern of eternal recurrence.

A red fox zigzags like an arrhythmic throb
in the inert vastness. Creature of undarkness,
fur buffed to flame sends a lick through my veins.
It bristles with purpose: mice, six feet below

the surface cower beneath its appetite.
My vapid slump stirs as it leaps high and dives
snoutfirst into the snow, scrabbles deep
till only its hindlegs show. I feel the blood beat:

I, too, could forage depths teeming with possibility,
gut each moment of promise, be present
to the boon of breath and body. Catch life
by the gullet as the fox makes its kill.

WHY I CLIMB MOUNTAINS

I dangle
over the jagged teeth
of rocks that bite
into the spines
of grown men
for sport.

My fingers are purpled raw,
pockmarking loose-skinned choss,
to seize on the sure bone of crags.

I reduce myself to staccato
gasps, sweating the measure
of all I am from the underbelly
of an overhang.

Like a carpenter ant
bearing its burden up pine bark,
I crawl up peaks
carrying my thudding heart
to the edge of cliffs so

I can thumb my nose at the abyss.

PATANGBAZI

My fighter tukkal tautens as the fan-tailed tawa
shadows me across the sky. Between us,

all the other kites—the parees and patangaas—
have spiraled to gutters, their shrapneled

heads speared and paraded by looting street urchins
while bhung-drunk jeers bay for more blood.

The bird of prey missiles at me. I jitter
in place and wait until the last five feet, then

roll a kamikaze loop around its papery contrail.
It flaps, a desperate rooster pulled

in for slaughter. My fingers slicken
as I reel, release, reel till my enemy's

thrusters rip from the strain and it nosedives
like a spent paper airplane. Grounded,

I unclench my palm from the sharded
twine that has carved me a new Life Line.

THE HOODED FALCON

The old falconer places a palm
under my elbow
to buttress the heaviness

of the shaheen's tethered
spirit, wild for wind and sky.

I am learning
to let beauty and terror
happen to me,

to lean beyond
my reach:

limits lie
at the end of time—
this world has no edges.

The falconer releases
the hood. My fear-
shut eyes open, meet

an executioner's stare
in the moment

before the falcon lifts
from me, winging
towards prey,

cleaving the sun
with a hooked beak.

ON BECOMING POLASEK'S "MAN CARVING HIS OWN DESTINY"

Much has been bared. Much
still remains: I am a sovereign
mind loosened from molds—
it was no slick birth

from a giving womb—
I fashioned flesh from stone,
carved my sinews,
whittled spine and bone.

Inch by inch, wrestled down
the flinty beast between my knees.
I must grind it to the ground
until it lies under my feet.

I am no marble god,
just a mortal bent to task,
scoring notches in my skin.
I build my marrow bit by bit,

every strike of cudgel and pick
shapes me to completeness.
Stony purpose at my core,
I will stand upon the floor,

smooth and sure like David.
Hardened from blows,
I am chiseling free and
until delivered whole, will keep

bringing the hammer down.

THE HOUSE I BUILT

I have taken a crowbar
to the graven paths
shackling me in place.
Swept shelves free
of gods, new and old,
their clutches empty
of the feathers they snipped
from my shoulders.

Ancestral molding cracks
and crumbles to sawdust,
as I pull screws
loose from the plugs
in my head. Nothing
is fixed—only
the frame remains—
like the beams
of a house condemned.

I glide through rooms—
unboxed, refashioned,
breathe
at windows wide
open for flight and
shake out the bare bones
of my wings.

GLOSSARY

ن	thirty-second letter of the Urdu alphabet. Pronounced noon

A

abhayāmudra	a hand pose in which the right hand is held upright, and the palm is facing outwards. It is the gesture of reassurance, safety and blessing in Hindu and Buddhist theology
allahu akbar	Arabic for "God is Great"
alif	first letter of the Urdu and Arabic alphabet, written as ا
Alif Layla Wa Layla	One Thousand and One Nights (The Arabian Nights)
azadi	freedom

B

Bamiyan	region in central Afghanistan
bhung	cannabis
Bollywood	Indian film industry

C

chador	shawl
charpoys	A bed consisting of a wooden frame strung with interlaced cords or webbing
chenar	oriental plane tree
chey	Eighth letter of the Urdu alphabet, written as چ
chowkidar	watchman
chunri	batik-like dyed fabric, characteristically bright, traditionally with complex patterns of small white squares
chutney	spicy condiment

D

dadi-ma	paternal grandmother
Dharmarajika	largest stupa of Taxila region and archaeological site
dhobi	laundry man
djinn	supernatural creatures in Islamic mythology as well as pre-Islamic Arabian mythology
dupattas	scarf
dhyāna	meditation

F

Faiz   Pakistani poet

G

gandhara   historical region in what is now Pakistan. The Gandhara
         civilization is known for its Greco-Buddhist art
gautama   Buddha
ghazal   poetic form composed of rhyming couplets
ghee   clarified butter used in South Asian cooking

H

hejazi   belonging to Hejaz, a region in ancient Arabia
hookah   water-pipe for smoking

J

jiddojohad   struggle
jharoka   balcony

K

kaaf   twenty-eighth letter of the Urdu alphabet written as ک
kaala dana   literally "black seeds." Name given to nigella sativa seeds

L

laam   thirtieth letter of the Urdu alphabet written as ل

M

maajhi   oarsman
maghreb   the time of sundown. Also means west
markhor   screw-horned goat
meem   thirty-first letter of the urdu alphabet written as م
mullah   Islamic cleric

N

naga   serpent deity, but also generically used for snake
nani-ma   maternal grandmother
nastaliq   name of the Urdu script
Noor Jehan   famous female Pakistani singer

P

paneeri	seedlings
parees	fairies
patangaas	moths
patangbazi	kite-fighting
podina	mint
pungi	a wind instrument with two reed pipes
purani haveli	literally "old mansion"

Q

qaaf	Twenty-seventh letter of the Urdu alphabet written as ق
Quran	holy book of Islam

R

rabab	stringed instrument like a fiddle
ragas	melodic framework in Indian subcontinental classical music
Ramzan	the Islamic month of fasting
Roznama Jang	A Pakistani newspaper. Literally translates to "daily war"

S

Sadeqain	Pakistani painter. Known for his calligraphy
sapera	snake-charmer
sardar	head of a clan or tribe
sari	length of cloth women wrap around themselves as clothing
sarson	mustard
shaheen	falcon
shajrah-nasab	family tree
shalwar	loose trousers worn by women in the Indian subcontinent
stupa	a mound-like structure containing Buddhist relics, typically the ashes of Buddhist monks. Used by Buddhists as a place of meditation
Sirkup	ancient Gandharan city and archaeological site
sufis	adherents of mystical Islamic belief and practice

T

tawa	a type of fighter kite
tey	fifth letter of the Urdu alphabet written as ت
tukkal	a type of fighter kite

U
urdu   a language of the Indian subcontinent

Z
zwad   twenty-first letter of the Urdu alphabet written as ض

ACKNOWLEDGMENTS

I am grateful to all the writers who have brought me to new ways of thinking and being. Who have opened my eyes to worlds through their stories and craft, and inspired in me the desire to share mine.

Thank you to Leah Huete de Maines, Kevin Maines and the Finishing Line Press editorial team for considering my manuscript and giving shape to a long-held dream. Christen Kincaid, my wonderful editor, for her guidance and encouragement throughout the process of publication.

My sincere gratitude to:
Jeffrey Levine, mentor extraordinaire, whose advice on writing and insights on my manuscript were invaluable.
James Longenbach, for being my adviser during Masters English.
Diane Smith, for giving me confidence.
Harris Khalique, for his kindness, brilliance, and literary sessions in Pakistan.
Alessandra Lynch, for being an inspiration.
Khayyam Mushir, for his friendship and being my first reader through the decades.

Most loving thanks to:
My parents, Dr. Azam Ali Khwaja and Shamsa Khwaja for giving me my first words and stories.
My brother and sister-in-law, Sajjad Ali and Farwa Naqvi, for their unconditional love.

Thank you to the Khwaja Mohammad Murtaza and Syed Abul Hassan Jafri clans, most especially my cousins Nadine Murtaza, Syed Hasan Mustafa, Abbas Mustafa, Sheena Najam, Asad Afzal, and Syeda Mehr Mustafa for always being there.
Kiran Zaidi, Supna Zaidi, Troy Peery, Shobi Zaidi, Mariam Rizvi for your love and unfailing support.
My kids, Zeyaan and Eva, for being my heart.

Finally, to my husband Wahaj Zaidi, my eternal gratitude and deepest love. Thank you for everything.

PUBLICATION ACKNOWLEDGMENTS

The following poems were originally published in these journals:

Alabama Literary Review: "Nastaliq"

Cutthroat A Journal of the Arts: "Silence Turning Shout"

Forge: "Sarson"

Grey Sparrow Journal: "The Mango Tree," "My Grandmother's Geese"

Menacing Hedge: "Fadings," "Crimson," "Jaddojohad," "The Hooded Falcon"

Pakistani Literature (by the Pakistan Academy of Letters): "Dancing Behind Closed Doors," "Writing on Water"

Pearl: "Burning of the Books"

Schuykill Valley Journal: "Dreamers of the Hills"

The Aleph Review: "Jharoka," "Unseen, Seen"

The Legacy Project (by SJC Bridges Out of Poverty): "Lore"

The New Guard: "Armor," "Lake Tapestry," "Giant Impact"

Willow Springs: "Stones Hold Water"

Zakia R. Khwaja grew up in Pakistan, in a household with strong traditions of written and oral storytelling. Both her parents are educators and she grew up reading Urdu, British and American literature. She went on to graduate with an MBA from Quaid-i-Azam University, Islamabad after which she worked in the nonprofit sector with microfinance institutions serving under-resourced communities. After she moved to the US, Zakia earned an MA in English from the University of Rochester, NY.

Zakia's work has appeared in *Grey Sparrow Journal, the Alabama Review, Forge, the Aleph Review,* and *Willow Springs* among others. She has served as a poetry instructor for Desi Writer's Lounge, an initiative for South Asian poets writing in English and given readings for the South Asia Free Media Association (SAFMA). She has also been published by the Pakistan Academy of Letters. She writes a blog at www.zakiarkhwaja.com on creativity and writing.

Zakia's poetry explores personal, cultural and political landscapes through the lens of her South Asian heritage. Her writing often melds Urdu and English, creating an alloyed voice that is a reflection of blended eastern and western literary sensibilities. Her poems celebrate culture but also invite us to spaces fraught with grief, charged with violence and tragedy.

When she is not writing, Zakia participates in marathon challenges and has a Guinness World Record for participation in the world's highest altitude road race. She loves traveling, collecting statuettes from different countries, and playing Scrabble. Zakia lives in Indiana with her husband and two children.